The White Stairs

Also by Jacquelyn Merrill Ruiz

The Swan

THE WHITE STAIRS

Jacquelyn Merrill Ruiz

Spear Stone Press
Cincinnati

The White Stairs

Copyright ©2015 by Jacquelyn Merrill Ruiz

www.jmerrillruiz.com

All rights reserved. No part of this book may be reproduced or transmitted in any form or by any means, or by any information storage and retrieval system without the written permission of the publisher, except where permitted by law.

Printed in the United States of America
First Edition

Book design and cover by Jacquelyn Merrill Ruiz
Author Photo by Adam Ruiz

ISBN 978-0-9963034-0-8
LCCN 2015908745

Spear Stone Press
Cincinnati
www.spearstonepress.com

for Adam, and for young me

Contents

ONE

Birth	13
Swimming Dreams	14
My Familiar is a Thief	16
Sleep	17
Rumblings	18
Hole	19
Santa Anas	20
The Sky Expanding	22
Cannibalism, for Vegans	23
Main Staircase at the Public Library	24
Ants, Falling	25
Brainworm	26
Wagons	27
Fine Print	28
Leaving Behind the Perfume Bottle in the Desert, or, Trying to Discard Myself	29
What an Entrance	30
Tragedy Attracts Them	31
Boundary Resistance	32
The Song We Danced to was "Moonlight Serenade"	33
Between Us and the Moon	35
Savanna	36
Release	37
My spirit is rough	38
Hera's Fog	39
A Love Song, for The Villain	40
Catch	41
Vision	42
Things to Never Tell a Woman	43
He doesn't write with sympathy	44

The Art of Arson	45
He called me what he called himself	48

TWO

Invocation of the Goddess Artemis, Upon Being Wronged	53
Sixty Names	54
The Night is a Page	55
Huntress lithe	56
Boomerang Returns Unexpectedly	57
Nostradamus Says I Have Five Years Left December 21, 2007	58
Paper Tugs	60
Order by Disorder from a Two Dimensional Spin Liquid	61
Indifference, Idolatry	62
Condensation	63
Hiding Beneath the Sun, the Seasons	64
Settlement	66
Overworked Employee in his Natural Environment	67
Time Makes Brutes	68
My Condition Hasn't Improved	69
The White Stairs	70
Defense	71
Namedigger	72
Storm Mosaic	73
Transmutation	74
Pinecones	75
Pioneers	76
Slip Up	77
The Tools to Back Down	78
The Opposite of Blushing	79
Calling	80
Passage	81

THREE
Keeping the Dead   85
Becoming a Child of the Night   87
I am the One Who Digs the Graves   88
Tir   90
The Dead's Departing Gift   91
School 21   93
The Bone-Carved Heart   96
Objects in Space   97
Impermanence is a Reputation that
      Precedes Me   98
Hunting Sandals   99
The sky is full of my mistakes   100
How to Carry the Moon   101
The Thrill is in the Chase   102
The Hunter's Kiss   103

ONE

Birth

I was a ghost for nine months.
My family could barely see me
silently stride across the floors.
My shadow shrunk. Streams of light
shone through me like a veil.
My laughter echoed empty off the walls
that swallowed every sign of life.
I was merely the true spirit of myself.

Even with all my effort,
something grew within me,
green and flesh and warm with fire.
Grew until its long neck
got caught in my tiny transparent throat,
and I choked it up and out.
I was sick for a long while,
but my offspring died
lying on the white rug. It couldn't live
outside me. It couldn't breathe the air.

Swimming Dreams

Lots of oceans, broken by my body
running from the shores of Santa Monica;
York, Maine; Northern Ireland.

My sisters are always there;
Once I grabbed my grandmother
by the shoulders and shook her.
My mother had to intervene.

The sun always blisters my skin,
I get salt in my eyes, and I hate
my wet hair
dripping down my back.

Always diving in to retrieve something.
Once I raced Lauren to a book.
Some slimy ocean thing brushed my foot, but—strangely—
I wasn't scared.
That's how I knew it was a dream.

Swimming pools show up too. One pool
expanded into the sky, and I swam
vertically: I wasn't afraid of the drain,
leaf-littered, and the sky grew
overcast and the wind
picked up. Pool-creatures often swim
sinuously beneath me.

Once I saved a boy from drowning
and nearly died. I stayed face-down
on the hot concrete, breathing hard,
loving the sun, seeing
beads of water on my arms, stringy strands
of hair splayed across my limp hand. I heard—
muffled—a man yelling at me.

The boy's father, devout Muslim,
was furious that I—woman, infidel, skin—
touched his son.

But the world was right again, stopped
shifting; it was summer in New England and
once I caught my breath, dove back in.

My Familiar is a Thief

Magic tricks turned by tiny hands—
mostly disappearing snacks and shiny objects.
It waits in woodland camouflage,
seedlike black eyes reflecting green,
pinpoint auroras hiding cleverness.
Nature's bandit, velvet-gloved, masked
and striped like a prisoner before the crime,
my hands are your hands, daintily
preferring cake and jewelry.

Sleep

The sun still spills a matchstick's length of light
over the cooling earth. I'm in the backseat
of Dad's car, body resting, head lolling
between the soft seat and warm glass,
my lethargy from sea salt.

This is the sleep every body deserves,
dreams of during interrupted nights.

A few minutes, ten, an hour—
even if it only happens once a decade,
it's enough time to connect
to the solitude
of the universe, hidden
in my ocean-pruned fingertips,
salt skin, sunburn—
Something in the sand I casually brushed
off my legs, that stuck to my toes,
the car mat. The slant
of orange dusk as we hit 60, 70 mph.
The engine hums. No one speaks.
The a/c chills like nothing felt
since autumn, but the day's heat radiates
from us like human stars—energy
that exhausted us, made us supple
for absolute sleep.

Rumblings

I guarded, quickly, that wet ink,
my vulnerable words—
so young, so new, such fragile things:
too soft, yet, for the world.

They must move gently, slow, and coy,
these things I'd never say.
My louder musings rattle lords
and chase success away.

Hole

There is a hole in my ceiling.
It's the size of a dinner plate
and twists
to the left
down a tunnel of stucco.

It's dark in there, and I try not
to open the cabinet it leads into
(or out from),
though I do keep
Tupperware on the shelves.

But even the containers revolt;
I find a sticky stuff on them. Maybe
from the hole.
I'm not taking chances.
I place them in the unused oven.

Now I have a huge useless cabinet
to hold my hole.
It has become the thing I hide and hide
from, afraid to find a grotesque living
or dying
or dead thing
there, or nothing.

Santa Anas

i. Banners have a mind of their own tonight,
trash in the streets
huddles in its filthy corners
and does not rise for the storm,
stubborn rubbish.
Cat-gray clouds slink across the moon,
bright and blown, too.

What chance do I have
when even the stars
obey the wind?

ii. Someone's cooking—potatoes, a pot roast.
Ratatouille.
This agitated weather brings me
chocolate chip cookies,
pizza from Umbria.
Chimneys puff scents of cedar,
frankincense, Great-Uncle Ern's pipe.

Thanksgiving's almost here;
I'm thankful for cold Los Angeles nights.
I shut my eyes and smell New England
October—
first frost, apple pie, hot chocolate.
Never mind I'm in a sundress.
I turn up the air conditioning,
snuggle under the down comforter,
nose running and frozen.

iii. Night slips in either way, careful
and chilly—a blonde spy
dressed in purple, clutching the walls,
trying not to make a sound.
Helicopters beat their wings between

the stars; flames lean on the hills,
ashes in my nostrils.

I wake up to the ember-colored morning,
throat itching.
It must be November.

The Sky Expanding

The golden grass tickles my neck,
purple flower heads lean into view
of my sky, a brand-new blue, clouds
electric white, cliffs mud-red and touching heaven.
Something buzzes, whirs, tries to distract
but I see my three bright souls
jump from the cliff and fall,
expand, float,
three dandelion seeds catching the wind
catching the sun
it's delight
a clear yellow noon—
they come to me, I open my arms and
they stumble breathless into me,
discarding the parachutes that brought them safely down.

Cannibalism, for Vegans

Strawberries. Pick them ripe
from a local farm. They're
as sinfully sweet as sucking on
fresh baby flesh.

Nectarine. Bite it slowly,
a sweet bum; stretchy, chewy
skin and fleshy sinews
get caught between your teeth.

Stanley plum. Kiss the skin,
hairless and loose over
the firm, testicle texture.
Buy them in pairs.

Orange. Rolled around,
it feels like a muscular bicep
or calf. Then,
the joy of peeling it.

Brussel sprouts. Steam them
just enough to give a supple exterior
and crunchy inside.
A bowl of little people-heads.

Main Staircase at the Public Library

Arrows bloomed in me, all alight,
all gasping in harmony—
knowledge is gold and white rapture,
hissing flames, the leafy reach—
Each one waving the others on,
each one earnest in its surrender.

Ants, Falling

I smash the words,
little bugs infesting my clean, white sheets.
Unafraid of death, they charge,
my ball-point flashes—slashes—
stops their little hearts,
word-guts galore in tiny explosions.
Like the ants, falling from between the beams
of the old lake cottage
onto my sisters' beds.
I let them have that room—I'd sleep
suffocated by the heat on the porch,
beneath starch-stiff children's sheets,
awaiting my own bug-fall.
That there was a solution
besides passing it on
didn't occur to me until the mess
was my own.

Brainworm

It measures my steps,
the inchworm in my brain—
a parasite
picking out each misstep,
deconstructing my failures
and spreading them out
like leaves across pavement.
Like a puzzle highlighting
my low times.
It's not all that dramatic,
in the context of my whole life,
but it eats at me, small-ly,
tiny bites out of my confidence.

Wagons

I fell off the wagon.
Many wagons, actually.
It's nothing as life-changing

as turning elephants into snails
and creaking through
the black of the map

to an X like a question mark
and the word
HOME.

My temperance was more like
an Oregon Trail
of Radio Flyers

leading to my salvation
of tire swings
and cotton candy.

This makes me
simple, my mistakes
manageable, my failures
forgiving, my wonder
unwavering.

Fine Print

I traveled West to reach my star
(the sky is lower there),
when NorthEast turned its back on me
and Hometown didn't care.

I ran toward those open arms
and recognition due—
not realizing the blinding sun
could so obscure my view.

While I forgot my troubles past
and danced in empty light,
reality, unnoticed, lurked—
its circle closing tight.

And after I had drunk my fill,
the West revealed the score
(my star no closer), turned me Home,
with memories, but poor.

Leaving Behind the Perfume Bottle in the Desert, or, Trying to Discard Myself

They marched me down the well-traveled road,
across the desert, across I don't know how many miles,
how many cities and towns, how many chances
to try to run away. Their excitement caught me up
and I stayed with them like flotsam in a wave,
though every time we stopped, I'd leave behind
my perfume bottle—the one thing I had kept—
until they asked me now if I carried it still
before we'd move on: they had to see it
before they'd turn toward our destination
before my father climbed atop the camel
and the winds snapped my black robes forward—
the earth, I suppose, also anxious for my arrival.
Still I couldn't remember the bottle, half-filled,
half-enjoyed but still so much potential,
as though I couldn't move forward
carrying the weight of those possibilities.

What an Entrance

So you thought love would just
walk up to you one day,
tap you on the shoulder and say,
"Excuse me, were you looking for me?"
And you'd take her hand and say, "Yes,
as a matter of fact," and go to an earthy café
to stare into each others' eyes, calm,
confident, at last complete.

Why is it love always comes to me
in the echo of a door slammed open,
like an agitated gust of wind,
groping me and swishing back
before I can recover?
Love introduces itself to me with shock,
a sense of violation, and the door
won't shut behind it. No way to protect myself,
always fearing it will come back
to take more stuff that doesn't belong to it.

I've tried to board it up, but I think
I secretly like it rushing in unexpected,
shoving its ghostly hand into my chest,
tugging at my heart just enough so I know—
it could kill me if it wanted, tear my heart
right out—and I'm so grateful for the tease
that I just open right up for it.

Tragedy Attracts Them

It wasn't until they could see my pulse
beat through my ribcage
that guys noticed me.

I am a shambled hut,
caved in without my innards,
lying underused,
stomach bruised and gaping.

Spirits find their way in there,
rush in with a snap
like the air-pop in cracked knuckles.

Swallowing shadows like air, reversed effect—
pares me down. I'm light and anchored.

Soul refuses the entanglement of food,
sprinting towards release,
its own scattering.

I always liked being bound.

Swaddled, cramped, crushed—
boundaries create me.

Self-pity is a useful tool,
self-confidence a privilege
of the non-single.

I'm used to standing alone.
I only want someone to lean on, to grab me
as I slip again.

Boundary Resistance

These ghosts don't say a thing.
They bang around the kitchen
while I sleep, destroying cockroaches,
silverfish as gifts for me
in the morning.

They can't answer my questions,
but I have to ask somebody.
I ask the impossible, anyway:
Why I'm the wrong end of a magnet
to him, so we're still drawn to each other
to a point, before our hands can't brush.

One day I'll lean in quick, see
if I can't make our worlds touch
when our lips do.

The Song We Danced to was "Moonlight Serenade"
(The instrumental version. No words.)

We were too close for me to stare at my shoes.
Because I couldn't look in your eyes,
I stared at your shoulder
and thought about my shoes—
white silk, five inch heels
and not high enough
to close the distance between our heights—
and how your hand was confident
on my back, high enough
to avoid indecency; low enough to say
I want you, too.

I can't remember why I couldn't look at you.
The music stopped.
I took your hand.

Sometimes when I'm doing dishes
and you stand behind me,
I forget who you are.
You shouldn't feel bad about this.
Sometimes I forget who I am, too.

And instead of looking at the dishes and soap bubbles
I'm staring at your shoulder again,
thinking about my white shoes
because the intensity of your stare would surely harm me.
Thank goodness the heels weren't higher,
or we may have been eye level.

The white carnation fell off your lapel.
I stooped to pick it up, since I was already
closer to the ground—we laughed—

pinned it back on but the damage was done.
Our eyes met.

I forget to put these things back
where I left them, they get lost
so when I see you across the dinner table,
or our hands touch in the movie theater,
I'm startled that I'm not alone anymore.

Between Us and the Moon

Smooth muscle shudders, shutting out
the edge so far behind, below—
lick my bruises, crushed lavender
and lemon juice
crumpled petals like bedsheets.
Dawn is too harsh.
Make mine moonlight,
blue and itchy,
I can't escape the tendrils
tender and kind,
whispers timid against skin,
your breath my only nightclothes.

Savanna

Our first Christmas tree
is pathetic.
We'd been buying mac & cheese
four for a dollar, each week for two months,
to buy the ornaments.
We got the cheapest tree they had—
something rejected by Charlie Brown
before he found something with a little more green to it.
Still it's too big for our meager decorations—
a dozen silver globes, a handful of heralding angels,
tinsel from the Asian market.
We plug in the lights.
I tie my knitted hat to the top branch,
where a star should go.
Now it won't be cold, I say.

Release

So desperate to release the tides,
the Seaweed Goddess strains.
To pull them in is laboring,
to keep them so, a pain.

How many heartbeats till the seas
are ready to go home
feels like a small eternity
that taxes to the bone.

But when it's time to loose the waves,
her earned crescendo breaks,
and none alive don't envy her
that sweet descent to peace.

* * *

My spirit is rough,
sandpaper stapled over crows' bones,
unapologetic in its ugliness.
But I've seen modern art.
Someone thinks it's beautiful,
provocative, deliberate.
Here I work the length of night
until the sun crowds out
the forgiving moonlight, demanding
to see what I've made
with its garlic breath and fleshy elbows,
inconsiderate prick.
His criticism is a bloodbath
masking hatred—
as though, in thirty-three years,
I never learned to recognize
discussion versus displacement.
I'll display the scars.
For all that, it's easy as falling
to ignore the fatty throngs.

Hera's Fog

So far from home, the night drips,
leaves shush the wind
that might help me find my way.
I can smell the invitation of a warm hearth,
just beyond—I'm not scared, just lost,
and eventually Apollo will drag the sun—
burning with indignation—with a rebel yell,
from one horizon to another.
But this is her way of telling me He's Not Yours,
a gentle if disorienting reproach.
She could kill me instead.
I'll wait for dawn, unless, before,
some bear or bull or owl pities me.

A Love Song, for the Villain

Your measured steps, uncanny calm, belies
the torment of your past. Control, long sought,
at last perfected. Now to torture cries
of pain and pleas from bloodied lips for naught
but vengeance boiled cold from years of rage
and helplessness. Why show restraint? Why flirt
with mercy, lest your heart be moved to stay
your blade from punishment that's rightly earned?
Nobody's innocent. You know you're right,
and what you do is for the greater good:
to maintain order, by reward or might
(though you embrace, whole-heartedly, the sword).
You're called Antagonist. I shouldn't fawn.
Misunderstood or evil, I'm undone.

Catch

Where is that chap? The gentlemanly
smile, the smell of tweed and rain—
wet dog.
Something else
undulates underneath—a sweetness
like honey, like chloroform, like ether—
is he trying to mask his own rot?

Gently trimmed beard, lifts his hat
out of duty.
Unbuttoned
in the dim lamplight of a Tiffany shade,
her own duty.

She notices the hook in his flesh,
a barbed J against his shirt—
he doesn't see.
She fears he will embrace her,
the point will catch her inner arm,
her tenderness pricked.

We all give up something for love.

Vision

Today my eyes swim
toward intrusion.
Voyeur-driven, lacked
inclusion, so set off down
that volatile path—
the uninvited, the witch,
the whore.
Babel, the storehouse
of miscellany,
misunderstood.
I never wanted it back, never
wanted to break
in, break trust.

Need for you rises in my throat
like bile, my stomach drops
so my hunger is between my legs,
my gut empty, empty
as the cold cellar
I fill with pictures of you.

Things Never to Tell a Woman

Love ended that night
you pulled me aside from our double-date—
the first and last—
and put your mouth so close to my ear
I heard your teeth click
beneath the raw whisper.
Words slipped in disguised—I half heard
because your thumb dug into
that tender place between my shoulder
and collarbone, and I was numb
and inundated with fever—the lights
expanded, everything sepia, and the cold
of Boston February rushed in.
Words burned my brain,
slid down my throat like whiskey
on an empty stomach.

That night you sliced my heart
like bread. You'd say its dark
like pumpernickel, or bitter
like sourdough.
Dark and bitter, I say,
sounds more like chocolate
or Guinness. Give me that any day.

* * *

He doesn't write with sympathy,
he has no use for lies.
His words will cut—a scalpel falls—
its subtlety belied.

He'll never comment on your work,
your mastery or wit—
his smallish brain can't process much
beyond your mouth and tits.

Though Critic of the Highest Rank
professes he to be,
your talent places last behind
his brave misogyny.

The Art of Arson

The dragon, the phoenix—
they're never chided
for their nature—the rumble
within, the lack of control.
If I were as fictional, as mythological,
I could join their numbers,
shrug at my damage and say,
"That is the nature
of Arsonist, as natural
as dragon or phoenix, as natural
as scorpion stings, as
brushfire and meteors."

It's one thing to bend
to your natural design,
and quite another
to shape your history
toward annihilation—

Fate never said, "You burn."
She said, "You build your burn."
So what if I build backward?
Spin my story to begin with destruction
and end in a flame-flicker—
calm catalyst.

Fate no longer owns me.
My destiny caught her skirt
and she lit up like cheap curtains.
There weren't even ashes left.

The murderer, the rapist—
he sees me bristle with heat
and turns away,
turns to find a victim at heart—

maybe Air or Water.
He denies me the struck match,
the struggle that will smother him—
he has his own desires to pursue,
his death in the far future—or never,
if he has his way.

One day I'll recognize the bloodied knife
behind his eyes and do the world a favor.
For now, I'm content to kindle.

I do regret the scars
I've inevitably etched
into those I love—
If they love me too,
sometimes I burn too bright,
and I blind; too hot,
and I singe.
Sometimes they like
to play with fire
and I forget their frailty.
Sometimes I forget
they will flinch from
my flame-tipped tongue,
my fire-wrapped fist.

Most difficult is falling in love—
especially with Earth, unmoving
as mountains. If he doesn't love me,
I try to pry the emotion out,
elbow-deep in muddy entrails.

I'd rather be beaten than ignored—I beat
myself with already-bloodied fists,
"Look, you cover me!" I shout through the smoke,
but he's already whole again.
I light my hair on fire, stamp,

burn myself out till I'm splayed on the ground,
steam rising from my tears—
another accelerant.

But I'll be up soon to follow—
to ask forgiveness and—if forgiven—
to burn us down again.

* * *

He called me what he called himself—
a rogue, a rake, a cad—
our differences of soul minute,
of body, more than that.
He recognized in me these traits,
he recognized my heart—
its eager blush for one more love,
another thrilling start.
I've waited for monogamy
to commandeer my head,
but each time logic dictates *one*,
I reach for three, instead.

TWO

Invocation of the Goddess Artemis, Upon Being Wronged

Artemis
your bow is swift
and I, your gentle acolyte,
do thee beseech—
extend your reach,
your bow of justice, bow of might,

amend the ill
his actions will—
my honor and my name defend.
To you I bow,
to cut him down,
and grant me justice, and revenge.

Sixty Names

to keep her sly, known by all,
slipping past unseen, the turning heads
catching the tail end of a midnight scent—
a silver thread of moonlight, crushed grass,
musk.

Her laughter is a name,
the whisper of an unloosed arrow,
little girls at play.

So many names, to know her from her brother—
as though the sun and moon
were too similar to tell—yellow disk, blue sky.
A burning golden chariot too easily mistaken
for his sister's pale, stag-drawn cart.

They suit her.
They spread her myth, so we can find her
in every corner, every tongue,
hiding in fairy tales, long ago and far away
from her home.
Even now, through years and miles,
she appears.

The Night is a Page

can never be torn out,
burned, forgotten

most people move
away from their adversaries,
lead normal lives—
hers are immortalized
constellations

directing us to never forget
consequences of justice
too swift

sky of enemies—
buckshot scattered by a bow, arrow
childish temper

most people send
scathing letters;
she's rewritten the heavens:
Artemis

Hunter and his Dog
Scorpion summoned to kill them
a fat mother-bear lumbering
home, face aglow, sweating
the smell of sex

full of guilt
she sends them to the stars

* * *

Huntress lithe,
through night you slice,
a laughing crescent doom—
the bowstring snaps,
your prey is trapped,
a panicked heart, a boon.

Boomerang Returns Unexpectedly

Three
mismatched suitcases, eight
cardboard boxes, and two
laundry hampers
followed me to my parents'
front door.
Car parked nose-out
on the driveway,
a quick getaway if necessary.
My childhood room
had become a library.

They'd given me everything
I'd need to go and stay away.

Dad opens the door for me anyway.

Nostradamus Says I Have Five Years Left: December 21, 2007

I know I can't see all the world
in that time, or experience
well, everything.

In many years, a newly minted man
may find my goal journal
heavy with empty check-boxes.
I don't know what yoga is, he'll say,
*or Swedish, or Petra, but she never
got to it, poor dear.*

I've considered a child and have lots of practice
setting myself up for heartbreak, but am certain
that creating life knowing that it won't live long
has similar Karmic consequences to selling your car
for twice its worth to someone who doesn't speak English.

I don't wonder anymore about love.
I feel like Whitman's twenty-ninth bather
in my unbound affection.

As for destruction, I hunted it once, with ferocity
like lust until it stained my every action
and everything I touched was ruined.
Once is enough.

Should I really reconcile my feuds,
turn against my own nature?
Will I die clinging to petty accusations,
or reveal my vulnerable innards again,
ripe?

I fear that I will die empty.
That I am already empty.

There are more human journeys than creation and hate.
I want them all checked off without regard
to what's outside me. How far can I go
into anything, just to experience, if
in sixty months none of it will matter?

What if it's closer to sixty years?

Paper Tugs

Each way, the paper tugs,
ribbons spinning off the spiral wire,
flecks falling like snowflakes
onto my black lap.
I tear out pages indiscriminately
and disregard nostalgia.
How many words I've thrown away—
words enough to build a book,
a library, a life.
Brushing the cats gathers enough fur
for tiny kitten clones,
and out in the world there are enough words
of mine in landfills
in cardboard boxes and toilet paper
for a chorus of tiny me's
to sing all the stories I wanted to forget.

Order by Disorder from a Two Dimensional Spin Liquid

The bottle sits up
like a lover from a one-night stand—
could be about to pee,
or grab his jeans and run.
Easy enough to get another—
bottle, lover, either—
what if he stays?
I couldn't tolerate the morning breath
every morning; or the abandonment
every night—pulling it close, desperate—
I forget which is worse—tolerance
or reverse-tolerance? Worst
is not settling for less, but craving
the less I've settled for.
Moderation's never been my style.
Addiction? Different story.
Luckily, my standards take shape
once I taste it. Like Johnnie Walker Blue—
first sipped out of a groomsman's flask. Later,
the groomsman, too. Lasted
as long as the liquor. Conned
so many times from surfacing flaws—
I'm careful now which vices
to fold into my heart; to nurse
one more night
in my dark, beating room.

* * *

Indifference, idolatry—
they're much the same to me.
No sooner than I find I'm loathed,
I gain a following.
If I were forced to waste my time
deciding whom to hear,
I'd never blossom, never know
my soul when it appears.

Condensation

I lived here once. Or maybe many times.
They run together now, the memories
of having hands, of pressing palms to doors
and window panes and walls—of using legs
to walk the fleshy rhythm. Heel-to-toe-
to-heel. How many faces have I worn?
What names have I responded to and earned?
This empty house is my exhausted lungs,
and I've forgotten every photograph
in every empty frame. I kiss the glass
to leave behind my love, my memory,
my handprint fading in the darkened hall.

Hiding Beneath the Sun, the Seasons

I no longer hear the world's pulse.
If I put my ear to the concrete, silent
and solid, I know it only swallows sounds.
Few places can I dig my fingers
into soft dirt, turn up grass blades,
bury myself until it's quiet enough
to hear the world spinning.

I miss puddles
to jump in, snowballs sliding down my shirt
to vulnerable skin. I miss bare trees
and leaf piles hiding moths.

I miss everything dead at once,
and the dying—I miss the chance
to regenerate; crocus poking out
of three inches of sleet.
Resurrection has lost its magic.

I'm close to the ocean
but afraid to visit, afraid
it won't make a sound, or
it's dried up or turned to pavement.

I don't know if there's motion anymore
or if everything stands still in a crater of dust,
sun baking heat fumes.
My throat's dry already—
That's part of my fever.
That's why I remember
four seasons, the sea—
so sick I can't lie down, I sit up
and rock to my own heartbeat.

So sick my heart pumps extra hard,
so hard it shakes me
like the moon shaking the sea,
waves rocking to the earth's pulse,
and spinning somewhere, dark Atlantic,
dogwood buds unfold in unison,
Orion ducks beneath the horizon,
and an undertow tugs a swimmer
                        into the earth's heart.

Settlement

No breeze to peel the paint strips
from their tenuous hold on the stucco—
a mottled soot-white and a pink
unlike a sunset or unbidden blush,
but akin to nuclear fallout and freshly burnt skin.
This is how they trick us.
Then we all get too tired
to repaint, repent, review.
Mom told me, "There is no paradise.
Photos of beaches, palms, you don't feel
the sand flies nip at your legs, or the humidity,
you can't smell the sewage that has nowhere to go."
A place's truth wears us down, we don't
forget it, we just forget
we once thought there would be more.

Overworked Employee in his Natural Environment

Twice, I saw Death. Not the act,
not body, not chemical reaction,
but the figure—hooded, shadow,
its skeletal fingers wrapped again and again
around the reins of terrified steeds,
breakneck speed, glancing back at the wake
of ripped-up hearts and slack jaws,
raw emotions pooling at our feet
and running unchecked into gutters.
It didn't look at us with pity or triumph,
or even a mild interest, but with the blank expression
we use when checking a hotel room
one last time, to ensure nothing was forgotten.
Empty sockets touched my gaze, turned, and fled on.
Not even a nod, a pointed finger,
no smile or evil laugh telling me I'm next.
Just the indifference of a hurricane,
the silent confirmation of a godless earth.

Time Makes Brutes

Time has taught me
we all become brutes
if we're patient enough.
Some people find nirvana,
but not from birth—
maybe they were bullies
on the schoolyard, maybe
crushed the head of a garter snake
on a dare. Then,
enlightenment.
There is not one person
who hasn't snapped
hasn't once been selfish
and there are many who develop a taste
for salty indifference.

My Condition Hasn't Improved

The whore's a wreck.
Divers driven into suffocation—
it was a bribe.
They should never have gone.

I can't ask them for tea,
but it's easy as breathing
to send them on errands dangerous
as diamond-mining, oil-drilling—
penetrating the earth.
Isn't that what men are good at?

The price of ambition is viability,
sick apples rotting
under tender moonlight—
the trickle turns to drips
and dries, throats closed from thirst.
The baby robins go hungry.

I've got to soothe this wound,
naked and unclotted.
I'll hemorrhage, I'm sure.

The White Stairs

Mud puddles fill,
my hands soft in them, feeling around,
pushing and sliding—

foul mirror.
That's not how I look.

Bright gold band through the gloom,
a ruddy ray of hope—marigold
and crackling—but no,
that's the thunder, torn
electricity, snapped whip.
It tingles.
I should be dead.

The white bells ring a song
from childhood—kiddie pools,
a sunroof, goldfish in a plastic bag.

Who am I to judge the gentle push,
the muzzle-nudge?
Better led in life than left behind.

Bring the knife—we'll cut the cake,
and I'll gnaw at my bonds
until my will breaks.

Defense

The black eyes of backed
into a corner,
empty rush as reason falls out
and hot wind brushes
angry up this rough stone chimney.

Crouched and craving, listening,
my mind grips knives—I'm sharp
and want to share. I've pared
reaction to its roots, discarded
logic (down below) and language,
kinship, civilized behavior.
I'm eyes and hands—
trajectory to a soft temple,
weighing the degree of danger,
likelihood of escape, statistics
that he'll strike again unfettered
when one well-placed blade
could smother future sorrow now.

Namedigger

Tell me the name
you hide in the crevices
of the places buried
so deep in you
their foundations are ancient
like a body thrown in concrete
and forgotten
until I come digging

Storm Mosaic

Here are the clouds, suckerpunch black
formed lightning-fast in my abyss—
that borderless rage
I throw hate into and rarely use—
the loose-change jar I forget about
until catastrophe, then find I'm rich.
I knew they were mine, I dragged them
from my toes—in that windless pastel sky
who else could conjure so much desperation
rolling straight toward us? He called it coincidence.
I called it my own and was afraid
to try again.

Transmutation

Shapeshifting never came easy.
I had to make myself a brick
and hold it
until I became an elephant,
my brow glazed in sweat.

Even now, only agitation
makes me flicker
like an A to Z flipbook,
antelope to zebra.

Now that I can do it easier,
quicker—I miss my own fingernails,
the reverse-birth-mark on my bicep.
I lose something
each time
I change to not-me.

Some things are difficult
for good reasons.

Pinecones

My creed is my own. Like pinecones
in winter, secrets tucked into pockets

and buried forgotten under a season.
I will not open for you. Perhaps you can guess

at my depths; perhaps you've known others,
think you know my hidden things

from blindly fumbling in your past.

This is different. We're each different.

I plant these beliefs at my chosen pace
and share as I please, gracefully meted out—

rationed smartly
for unknowable rough futures.

Pioneers

Balloon rides, cowboy spurs—
How can people settle on the earth
when dust can't? Kicked up
by wind and hooves, thick boots,
running child-feet, the farm cat—
the one they didn't drown.
What a life to be saved for—
wretched mice and toast crusts.

Is it any wonder we wish to fly?
Thrum out the theme of a windmill life,
the tattered drum. The bear's pride
resides in our hearts, too.
The chicken shrieks.

If only this corset weren't so tight; if only
I knew how to be barefoot and helpless.

Slip Up

It's a talent to walk
across floors so polished, across carpets
so soft,
upright,
when it's all designed to tilt
toward a waiting cage.
And it's painful, more painful
than pine needles on packed dirt,
rough roots, not watching
where my foot falls.
I'm waiting for it to transform,
I'm waiting and biting my lip
to keep these screams inside,
shaky footsteps in a hallway slick with blood
like a slaughterhouse
like the decks of whaling ships
so easy to lose my grip
and give in to the reaching darkness.

The Tools to Back Down

My desperate, ardent wish: not fulfilled,
but tools placed in my grasp. A chink, a clue,
a giant arrow sign outlined in lights
all blinking "Here, look here!" Then use your brain
to fill in blanks, that dirty, restless mind
that worries vengeance like a thumb-smoothed stone,
and drops it, dulled, but known, into a pool.
I try to teach myself to let it go.
My temper's always been too quick, too welcome.
I've been trying not to start a fight.
Perhaps this is the chance I need, a chance
to make a ruin, or to understand
that burning is a choice, that I could walk
away from it, if I could teach my feet
that lofty coward's dance.

The Opposite of Blushing

Falling sideways, falling home,
the best thrills are anticipation and uncertainty.
Fear is a wet, sucking pop—then nothing.
I wasn't always like this, this piecemeal nightmare
of mixed media, crows' bones and paper towels.
I touched the world light as fireflies
and glowed as dim, romantic and blushing.
Now I'm metal edges and maggots,
ripe and rotting beneath
a naked lightbulb.

Calling

Men can't spell my name
in any alphabet—sticks
or trees, dashes, pictures—
How do you spell a gust of wind?

Pick up the lines of old fairy tales—
hiccup, another breadcrumb—
Snow White's shriek,
the old witch's cackle.
Two heads to every woman—the mother
whose womb grows full; the monster
those hormones create.
Might as well wait
till the next full moon. You'll find me
reflecting in a silver stream—
one image in a holy glow, the Other
growling in the brush.

Passage

Tripped up little tramp,
full moon, the belly's grown into a bulge,
and who can stop that?

Gladly I throw the jewels glittering
like razors, tiny shiny razors—
emerald and amethyst.

The stone alley is shadowed
in that moonlight—
a snake in the woven basket,
red-ringed and domesticated.
And those eyes—those glowing eyes
beneath the darkened hood.

I don't want to wait but this is where the donkey stopped.

The men wait—patient snakes;
jaguar stalks its prey. Circling
the sacrifice—the beaten bull.

Inhuman things, their blood runs in pulses
attached to sense of smell.
They like the smell of fear. They tear
the horns from the bull and I am lost.

THREE

Keeping the Dead

harvesting pomegranate seeds
like digging to the underworld—

I peel back the crust,
roll out the arils, tender,
and tough rubies

I can't articulate why
this is like descending
a muddy staircase, moving
into the earth not rotting
yet—

dirt on my hands
in my mouth
it smells clean—fresh
but the sod walls
are built with blood

every seed is perfect, robust—
I can't help eating them all
and lighting two candles:
one orange like the dying stalks
for the dying summer gods,
one black as midnight—
the door
for the dead

now I'm warm.
I tell the spirits they're welcome—
the gods twist their flame
but those who have passed
are still—

I ask for the death of my withered parts
and always forget that it is steady
—not a flash—
fasting without end
uncertainty
planting seeds in barren earth
and waiting

Becoming a Child of the Night

He told me that it wouldn't hurt—
that pain's a human thing.
That by the time I recognize
the feeling, I'd be free.

So gentle, so adoring, he—
immortal, like a god—
I yielded to his stunning grace,
his cold embrace, his love.

How long ago he took from me
my life, I cannot tell.
Each night since then is sanguine bliss.
Each night since then is hell.

I am the One Who Digs the Graves

The shovel was already out,
flirting with the idea of rust
as rain teased it, off and on.
Two holes dug for two anonymous plants.
All I knew, bees loved them—
my only request as I pushed the empty cart
down aisle after aisle of yet-unflowered shrubs.
Why own anything without another purpose?
Why not
save the world, too?

I knew her rabbit had died,
like when I know there's trouble ahead,
an unseen storm chasing these fast white clouds.

And there's the part of me, reluctant,
that had to be taught to react
correctly to life situations,
and when tragedies unfold, I hit that default switch
and find myself saying things
a compassionate person would say, promising things
that sound right, though they're a burden
to me.

I finished digging the third wound
I'd make in the earth that day
before she arrived.

It was an invitation to consider mortality

but I only thought, I will always be
a gravedigger now.
And hasn't that always been my role.
To dirty my artist hands with earth,

to step down and sully myself,
force my mind to recognize
my body lives, too, in a world outside?
It's a show. To deflect suspicion, to avoid
eyes, spotlight, a quiet hospital—
scared of being detected, I volunteer
the work most physical, I volunteer
the tasks from which others shirk.

I am the one who digs the graves.

Tir

This land is like my life—so bare and red—
no flesh to keep me company, save
my metal, living weapon. And the dead.
I used them for the thrilling fight they gave.
My heartbeat is a steady drum of war,
and courage cleaves to beads of sweat. My breath,
so warm to me, is often taken for
a cold breeze—a gust of impending death.

They call me death. They see my sword and shield,
both stained with blood, and do not think, "Here comes
a valiant hero!" Rather, "Did she kill
my kindred?" And my infamy is sealed.
I walk my path. My murder never numbs.
At least they don't believe I have free will.

The Dead's Departing Gift

crossing through our yard
icy grass pricks
our insteps; we giggle,
draw quick breaths
trying to keep warm
and quiet

orange glow of carved pumpkins
in the distance leads
pirates, princesses, ghosts
    away from our footsteps   falling
steadily toward the clearing

it's darker here than in any haunted house
but is only haunted
 itself
when we invite them
    three witches, three sisters   calling
the dead from their side
of midnight's thin veil

moon nearly full
the brightest stars eclipsed
by its crisp light
farmers, astrologers
call it the bloodmoon

we watch it with the frozen ground
beneath our backs
    we whisper secrets   ask the dead
to sing us lullabies
wait until dawn

    until we can see our white breath
tinted rose by the sun
our new friends fading vapor

School 21

i. The bed frame sags
with forty years of rust,
every day, in the middle of its yellow room,
shackles dangling toward the ancient linoleum
still stained with blood.

And at the head of it, a giant photo—
its last prisoner, bled out
in black and white, where the bed still stands.
It's a comfort
to see it instead of imagining something worse,
the something worse in the next building,
the gallows in the courtyard, the fields
an hour away, where blank-faced soldiers
swung newborns by the heels.

I back out of the room in silence,
hands clasped behind me. We shuffle
into the next room, identical,
but for the body's position in the photo.

Outside, three barrels beneath a wooden beam.
To read the sign translated to English,
I avoid stepping on the weeds
pushing through cracks in the walk.

Just as I think, surprised,
that I haven't felt haunted,
my knees buckle and—
embarrassed—
I pretend I tripped,
though I stay kneeling
as my shaking hands unscrew the water bottle.

ii.	The last building is a maze
of brick hallways and cells,
cramped and hot,
winding through hundreds, thousands
of prisoners' photos, all the same—
black and white glossies, like headshots.
I can't photograph them.
After the heads, the skulls.
Locked in glass and packed as tight
as prizes in a claw machine.

Then I feel them.
Pushing through cracks in history,
like the weeds, like the villagers
just trying to make it through the lean season,
too busy surviving to play games of power.

It's a mistake to let them in, a mistake
to release my grasp on the veil
I'd been clutching to myself, afraid,
but there's no one else
or I would have seen her, sobbing,
I would have seen him, running
from these rooms full of ghosts
into the country full of them.

And my fear
that I'll take them all home with me
turns to revelation:
I must take them home with me.

iii.	In the last room, an elevated Buddha
looks past the cabinets of bones,
out the door, to blossoming trees
and stubborn grass.

My still-shaking hands slip riel into a tiny glass box,
raise three incense to a plastic lighter,
and plant them smoking in the bowl of sand.

I acknowledge you.

When I turn to the door,
two women who also stayed behind
rush to light their own incense.

The Bone-Carved Heart

Running over delicate decay
my invisible fingers
finger the cold rot, the marble coolness—
was it carved to be hollow, a scrimshaw
masterpiece,
or did it bloom empty?

I thought darkness would be dim
and quiet, a place unspeakable
untouched by light. A secret buried
under all this flesh, these dark organs,
unyielding bone.

It's easier to touch than I like
and bathed in light like nebulae.
The hard line that was supposed to separate
good and evil so distinctly
is only a thin film,
like the surface of soured milk.
Walking from one to the other
as easy as entering another room.

I thought it would hurt more
but death is already shaped in our hearts.

Objects in Space

The universe sighed,
star systems sailed through the nothing—
toy boats in a bathtub—
and rested in their orbits.

Birch trees lose leaves by yellow fistfuls
until one windy autumn evening. Next morning,
naked branches shiver, silver. It stands center
in its cast circle.

It's only an object.

A pistol is an object
like a branch.
Both could be benign.
Both could take a life.

Dust pollen and galaxies.

Anything could kill us,
scatter our parts like stars.

Impermanence is a Reputation that Precedes Me

If I asked you to think of me
in trying times or shining skies,
you'd see me as a wisp. Whispering,
a steam ghost over sewer grates
at 4AM, after the rain. The thin cloud
stretching
stretching so the blue shines through
and I disappear like breath on a windowpane.
I'd fade.
I want no monuments. Minimalist,
not even a marker—
I'll die again when it cracks, eroded,
broken. Once is enough.
Rather, hear my laughter in that distant rumble.
I'll sneak up on you, suddenly,
or you'll keep a watch, expected
dark cloudheads on the horizon
following a straight line. Why bother
with ready-made paths? Nimble,
stepping over obstacles, a dance,
a show of lights. I'm such a ham.
A promise and a tease.
I pop your ears, tickle and drench.

Remember me in thunderstorms.

Hunting Sandals

Sliding my feet into the leather, soft
from centuries of use, shaped by persistence
to fit only me. Slowly, adjust. Curl my toes.
Thin laces look like tiny snakes, struck dumb,
too long, paralyzed in the silver light—
hiss between my tugging fingers, the rasp of old women
whispering as they spin, measure, snip.
One across the other, climbing higher, to my knees.
I braid in the moonlight
tradition and unknown, what's built
and what may be, knotted
indiscernible and tight.

* * *

The sky is full of my mistakes.
I've read it a million times, and some nights
I forget, cheeks flushed from the hunt,
laughing into the exhaling darkness.
Other nights, I wish I had a trench coat
to tie around me too tightly, shove hands
trembling with anger into deep pockets,
so I can mumble my regrets
and give the heavens dirty looks.

How to Carry the Moon

Apollo rushes to his horizon, all sweaty and golden
and smiling, still shouting exuberance
for the rush of pulling that gaudy orb.
As if it were a fifth horse, stallion
and incalculably valuable. It's an eyesore
and makes me pink and itchy.
There's something to be said for subtlety.
I pack the moon carefully,
in velvet, in cobwebs,
carry it in my arms to my horizon
breathless and barefoot—I only start walking,
and release.

The Thrill is in the Chase

The stag and bear
run ahead. They know
I'll find them—my gift
is of nature, feeling out the land
and beasts. I have eyes everywhere,
hands on every blade of grass,
pulse on the stones, in the earth—
I run ahead of the animals
that run from me.
The grove extends from my arms
like the arrows from my bow—
that sudden thud of meeting its mark.

That's where my pleasure ends.
I'd spare their lives if I could.

I laugh as I ride, branches catching
my hair, cheeks red from the pace,
the wind, my joy.

I hunt alone.
My chaste nymphs prefer the silver pool,
showers of pink blossoms,
daisy wreaths.

The only blood I let them see
is their own,
when I fly the full moon across the sky.

The Hunter's Kiss

for Iphigenia

Men are cruel and unpredictable.
I must have known this, somewhere buried

in the dark flesh of my heart,
when I begged God to keep me
a virgin. I was two. Barely
housetrained, I knew enough
about the complications of sex
to keep me off of it forever. You know.
Take a look at my relatives.

Your father killed my pet.
Maybe the rapture of the chase—
just him, his horse, the ten-point stag—
filled his veins with obsession.
Maybe he didn't recognize the forest.
I will not take the blame for this passion:
I did not incite it. Not against
my own creature, not in my own woods.
This is not the hunt I nurse
in the groins of men.

He took it from me—the joyous flight,
the grove, my stag.
The clever fool took the arrow
he snapped into my beast's heart—the arrow
in Mycenaean colors that sang
its archer's identity.
This alone is enough
for me to draw my own arrow.

He spent too much time drinking,
pouring sacrifices to the gods

he thought would benefit him most.
He forgot humility.
He forgot the wrath of women.
He forgot that he was mortal.

His life wasn't mine to take—
a man for a deer? Father
would never allow it
(and he allowed me much).

So I denied him the wind.
I told him he'd used it up
running through my forest,
hunting what wasn't his.

Oh, he was furious! Such a simple thing
to deny a mortal man,
but what an impact! I delighted
in his torture—the ships
were already packed with olives
and cheese, shields and vambraces
and sword-strapped soldiers.
Stuck at the docks.

It couldn't last—everyone had something at stake,
and the gods owed your father favors.

If he had learned his lesson,
apologized to me—
turned his heart inside-out—
I'd release his winds.

But men are cruel and unpredictable.

Believe me, if I had known
the price of revenge—
bound, soft and white—a lamb—

your virgin blood
dripping down the altar stairs...

Your brother tried to stop it.
He said your name as they slit your throat—
he gave you humanity
when every man made you a beast.
To your father, you were more precious
than any magnificent stag
in any enchanted grove—
breath left your lungs
and became the wind he wanted.

I reminded your mother how she called to me
as she stood on the blocks
birthing you, begging me for relief
and your safe arrival.

She wept. I wept beside her—
a shadow, a whisper—
giving substance to her memories.

I only asked her to remember,
remember.

She sent your father to follow
where he sent you,
sent my pet.

I want to believe he found you again,
folded his face into your arms,
wept for you, too.
But I can't hear beyond this world.
And what insight could he have gained about life
among the dead?

Know you were avenged. Know I think about you,
every evening, drawing you in the stars,
pure priestess, restless sacrifice.
It is for you I lead the moon.

About the author

Jacquelyn Merrill Ruiz was raised in New England, forged in Los Angeles, and embraced by Cincinnati. She's written all manner of genres for years, but it was her poetry that earned her the coveted Master of Professional Writing at University of Southern California. Her most recent book, *The White Stairs*, is a poetry collection rooted in transformation. She currently lives in Ohio, where she toasts the full moon with kombucha and gathers thunderheads for later use.

Find out more about the author online at
www.jmerrillruiz.com

www.ingramcontent.com/pod-product-compliance
Lightning Source LLC
Chambersburg PA
CBHW020945090426
42736CB00010B/1272